Christopher Columbus

T0102560

Samantha Bell

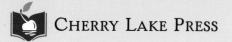

CHERRY LAKE PRESS

Published in the United States of America by Cherry Lake Publishing Group
Ann Arbor, Michigan
www.cherrylakepublishing.com

Reading Adviser: Beth Walker Gambro, MS, Ed., Reading Consultant, Yorkville, IL
Content Adviser: Heather Bruegl, M.A. (Oneida/Stockbridge-Munsee) Historian-Indigenous Consultant-Lecturer

Photo Credits: © RicSou/Shutterstock, cover, title page; © Arcady/Shutterstock, 5; © Rudra Narayan Mitra/Shutterstock, 6; © agsaz/Shutterstock, 7; © Nomad_Soul/Shutterstock, 8; © joserpizarro/Shutterstock, 9; © BlueOrange Studio/Shutterstock, 10; Girolamo Benzoni, Public domain, via Wikimedia Commons, 11; © Arsgera/Shutterstock, 13; © Venturelli Luca/Shutterstock, 14; © Chris Harwood/Shutterstock, 15; © Everett Collection/Shutterstock, 17; Benson John Lossing according to the source, but there is the signature of William Z., that may be William Barritt, who made engravings with him., Public domain, via Wikimedia Commons, 18; Library of Congress, Public domain, via Wikimedia Commons, 19; L. Prang & Co., Boston, Public domain, via Wikimedia Commons, 21; Lewis W. Hine (Life time: 1874-1940), Public domain, via Wikimedia Commons, 22; David Wilson, CC BY 2.0 via Wikimedia Commons, 24; George Grantham Bain Collection, Library of Congress, Prints and Photographs Division, 25; Smithsonian American Art Museum, Museum purchase, 27; Andres Sonne/Shutterstock, 28; James.Pintar/Shutterstock, 30

Cherry Lake Press is an imprint of Cherry Lake Publishing Group.

Library of Congress Cataloging-in-Publication Data has been filed and is available at catalog.loc.gov.

Cherry Lake Publishing Group would like to acknowledge the work of the Partnership for 21st Century Learning, a Network of Battelle for Kids. Please visit http://www.battelleforkids.org/networks/p21 for more information.

Printed in the United States of America
Corporate Graphics

Note from publisher: Websites change regularly, and their future contents are outside of our control. Supervise children when conducting any recommended online searches for extended learning opportunities.

Samantha Bell was born and raised near Orlando, Florida. She grew up in a family of eight kids and all kinds of pets, including goats, chickens, cats, dogs, rabbits, horses, parakeets, hamsters, guinea pigs, a monkey, a raccoon, and a coatimundi. She now lives with her family in the foothills of the Blue Ridge Mountains, where she enjoys hiking, painting, and snuggling with their cats Pocket, Pebble, and Mr. Tree-Tree Triggers.

CONTENTS

CHAPTER 1

The Story People Tell
The Man Who Discovered America

Christopher Columbus was born in Genoa in 1451. Genoa is part of Italy today. Italy was not a united country back then. Genoa was on the coast, and Columbus grew up with a love for the sea. For a while, Columbus worked with his father weaving wool. He also studied mapmaking and sailing. Columbus eventually left Genoa to sail with a fleet on the Mediterranean Sea. When his ship wrecked off the coast of Portugal, Columbus set up a business as a mapmaker and bookseller.

For a long time, Europeans had been trading with Asia for goods such as spices, ivory, and silk. The easiest trade route was through the Middle East. The trade route was

A view of Genoa, Italy, where Christopher Columbus was born

over land. It was called the Silk Road. Western European nations were Christian. Middle Eastern nations were Islamic. Christian armies fought crusades against Islamic nations. The nations were **hostile** to each other. Islamic nations cut off European access to the Silk Road. Demand for Asian spices and goods was still high. Europeans began looking for a different way to Asia. Columbus believed he could reach Asia by sailing west across the Atlantic Ocean.

The story of Columbus said that he had an idea that no one else had. It says he was the only one who thought Earth was round. No one believed him. Columbus was determined to prove them wrong. But he did not have a ship, a crew, or the funds for the trip.

Many royals turned Columbus down. They didn't want to financially support his trip.

During the 15th and 16th centuries, the rulers of several European countries were paying for expeditions. They wanted to find riches and unclaimed lands. Columbus presented his plan to Portugal, Spain, France, and England. They all turned down his request. But for Columbus, the trip was about more than just finding

Spreading Christianity to Asia was one of Christopher Columbus's goals for his trip.

a trade route. He also wanted to spread Christianity to Asia. Columbus went before King Ferdinand and Queen Isabella of Spain a second time and then a third time. They finally agreed to finance his trip. After 7 long years of trying, Columbus was finally able to go.

Columbus set sail from Spain in 1492 with three ships, the *Niña*, *Pinta*, and *Santa Maria*. According to his calculations, the trip should have taken 2 weeks. But after more than 2 months, there was still no land in sight. Columbus told his crew to keep going. But the men thought they might run out of supplies. They began to talk of **mutiny**. Columbus bravely stood up to them.

The *Santa Maria* was one of Columbus's ships for his voyage in 1492.

The story says that Columbus was a skillful **navigator**. He just needed more time. Columbus asked for 2 more days. On the second day, one of the sailors spotted land.

On October 12, Columbus and his crew came to an island in the present-day Bahamas. He named the island San Salvador. The men explored San Salvador and traveled to some of the other islands. Columbus was sure these were the islands in the east known as the "Indies." He did not realize he was on a very different continent.

THE IMPORTANCE OF MATH

Around 240 BCE, Greek scholar Eratosthenes figured out a way to estimate Earth's **circumference**. His estimate was close to the actual measurement. But Columbus did not believe it. He thought Earth was smaller. That was why he was certain he could sail to Asia in 2 weeks. It was why he was convinced he had reached Asia. Math was also the reason that nobody believed him. Almost everybody in 1492 knew the world was round. They just also knew it was much bigger than Columbus thought.

The Taíno people were historically an Indigenous people group of the Caribbean.

Columbus met the **Indigenous** people of the Caribbean. Because he thought he was in India, he called them "Indians." He returned to Spain with a little gold, some birds, and plants from the islands. People soon realized that Columbus did not land in India. The king and queen were excited about his discoveries. More Europeans would soon be sailing west. Columbus had opened a new route to explore and colonize.

CHAPTER 2

The Facts of the Matter

In Search of a Trade Route

For many people, Christopher Columbus represents the heroic bravery and perseverance of explorers. But the real story of Columbus in the Americas has a very different tone. Columbus was the first European to land on the Caribbean islands. But he was not the first person to discover them. The islands were already inhabited by millions of Indigenous people. For these islanders, Columbus's arrival marked the beginning of the end.

Columbus and his crew set sail in 1492 on the three ships. When they landed, Columbus met the Taíno people. They called their island Guanahaní. Columbus ignored this name and renamed it San Salvador. The Spanish explored islands in the Caribbean for 3 months. He called one island

Many people of Taíno descent keep Taíno traditions alive today.

The Taíno people already called this island Ay-ti. Christopher Columbus decided to rename it Hispaniola.

Hispaniola. The Taíno called it Ay-ti. This island is the location of present-day Haiti and the Dominican Republic.

Everywhere he went, Columbus used force against the Indigenous people. He and his crew searched for gold. They killed people. They enslaved people. They thought because they were European and had guns that they had a right to the land and resources.

On the way back to Spain, the *Santa Maria* hit a coral reef off Hispaniola. With the help of the Taíno, the crew used the ship's wood to build a fort. They named it La Navidad. Columbus left 39 men at the fort. But he decided to take some of the Taíno back with him. He wanted to show the Spanish king and queen that

A MESSAGE IN THE SKY

In 1503, Columbus was stranded in Jamaica for a year. After months, the Indigenous people stopped giving the explorers any food. They were not getting anything worthwhile in trade. But Columbus knew from his **almanac** that a **lunar eclipse** was coming. He told the people that his God was angry at them. To prove it, the moon would "rise inflamed with wrath." The night of February 29, the eclipse made the moon dark and then turned it red. The islanders were terrified. They offered Columbus food and begged for mercy.

the people could be enslaved. He kidnapped at least twenty of them. Only six to eight survived the trip across the ocean.

Columbus told the king and queen about the islands. They were pleased and paid for a second trip in 1493. This time, Columbus was to set up Spanish colonies. He took 17 ships and more than 1,000 men. Columbus returned to La Navidad. But the fort had been burned. All of the men had died.

Columbus kept sailing along the coast of Hispaniola. He started a new colony called La Isabela, named after the queen. Columbus served as the colonial governor. Columbus was not a good **administrator**. War soon broke out between the Spanish and the Indigenous people. The Spanish had more advanced weapons. Many Indigenous people were killed. Even more were captured and enslaved. They were forced to search for gold. European diseases also took their toll on the Indigenous people. In just 5 years, two-thirds of their population was wiped out. Columbus was called back home in 1496.

On his third voyage in 1498, Columbus left with six ships. Three ships sailed for Hispaniola with supplies. Columbus took the other three to search for more new lands. They were the first Europeans to see South America.

A painting of Christopher Columbus by Sebastiano del Piombo

Columbus was arrested in Hispaniola
for mismanagement of the colony.

They explored the coast until Columbus's health began to worsen. Returning to Hispaniola, he discovered the colony had turned against him. Columbus was eventually arrested for mismanagement of the colony. He returned to Spain in chains, although he was freed 2 months later.

Columbus convinced King Ferdinand and Queen Isabella to send him to the Americas one last time. He still believed he had reached Asia. Now he wanted to find a **strait** linking the Indies with the Indian Ocean. In May 1502, he set sail with four old ships and 140 men, including his brother and his son. But the voyage had troubles from the start. The crew faced a hurricane, storms, and strong **headwinds**. They moved into Central America, but they could not find the strait. The ships became stuck because of a low tide. Local Indigenous people attacked it. Termite-like worms ruined the ships. Columbus's men turned on him again. He returned to Spain in 1504. The expedition was considered a failure. He died 2 years later.

CHAPTER 3

Spinning the Story

The Making of a Hero

One reason the image of Columbus as a hero became so popular was because of a book. In 1828, author Washington Irving wrote *A History of the Life and Voyages of Christopher Columbus*. He wanted to write a historical account. But he also wanted to encourage a feeling of patriotism. America was a young country without a lot of history. But Columbus was part of that history.

Irving also wanted to write a great story. To make it more exciting, he made up some information about Columbus. For example, Irving said that Columbus was the only person who believed Earth was round. But the Greek mathematician Pythagoras proved it around 500 BCE. Many other ancient Greeks agreed. In Columbus's day, most educated people believed Earth was round.

A work of art depicting Columbus's landing in "the new world," titled
Columbus Taking Possession of the New Country

Thousands of Italian immigrants arrived in the
United States starting in the late 1800s.

Later, Columbus actually gave up his round Earth idea. Because of his navigational readings, he decided it was shaped more like a pear.

Before 1750, not many people celebrated Columbus. But in the 1800s, history books started focusing on role models. Irving's story of Columbus was a perfect fit. In the book, Columbus was determined and ambitious. He persevered when things became bad. He overcame many obstacles. Irving mentions the mistreatment of the Indigenous people. But overall, the book is positive.

This view of Columbus as a hero soon became very important to one group of Americans. In the late 19th century, thousands of Italian immigrants began arriving in the United States. Most of them were poor farmers looking for a better life. However, many Americans did not welcome them. The Italian immigrants had darker skin and hair and often did not speak English. Many Americans thought they were untrustworthy. They thought they were criminals. Newspaper articles reinforced this image. These feelings encouraged widespread discrimination and even violence against the Italians. In 1891, 11 innocent Italians were killed by a mob.

The Italian Americans worked to overcome the negative **stereotypes.** They began to identify with Christopher Columbus. After all, he was a hero and the most "American" of Italians. He played a key part in the history of the Americas by introducing Europeans to these continents.

A HERO TO RELATE TO

In 1892, some members of New York's Italian American community had an idea to overcome negative stereotypes. The 400th anniversary of Columbus's first voyage was in 1892. The nation would celebrate with the 1893 Chicago World's Fair. Italian Americans raised $20,000 for an Italian sculptor to create a statue of Columbus. New York politicians wanted to hide the statue in the Italian part of the city. But Italian American leaders convinced them to place it in a corner of Central Park. The statue was installed on October 12, 1892.

Soldiers march in a Columbus Day parade in the early 1900s. It was seen as a day to celebrate Christopher Columbus as a hero who discovered America.

In 1892, President Benjamin Harrison created Columbus Day in response to the violence against Italians. Columbus was helping Italian immigrants find their place in American society. Columbus Day became a national holiday in 1937. In 1971, it was first observed as a federal holiday where banks, schools, and government buildings were closed.

CHAPTER 4

Writing History

Gathering Sources

Historians have detailed records to use for discovering what really happened on Columbus's voyages. These come from several different sources. One of the main sources is Columbus himself.

Columbus kept a detailed journal during his first voyage. He wrote about the land, the weather, and the wildlife the crew saw. He recorded the moods of his crew. He wrote about his first impressions of the Taíno. When Columbus returned to Spain, he gave the journal to Queen Isabella. She had a copy made and gave it to Columbus.

Columbus also wrote letters. After his first voyage, he sent one to the king and queen. Copies were made for the court officials. The letter was a way of announcing Columbus's discoveries. He told them about the Taíno

A painting of Columbus and Queen Isabella of Spain by artist Peter Frederick Rothermel

Columbus's letters to the king and queen of Spain were copied and distributed to court officials during his voyages.

and their culture. He included an argument that the Taíno would be easy to conquer. He said it would be easy to enslave them. He talked about how they were physically fit and did not have weapons. They were also timid and fearful. It would be easy to make the Taíno do whatever the Spanish wanted. He mentioned some of the other tribes, too. Columbus sent a similar letter to his friend and sponsor Luis de Santángel. This letter was printed and spread throughout Europe.

In his next letter to the king and queen, Columbus outlined his plan for setting up colonies on the islands. He talked about how they should be governed. He mentioned what they would do with the gold they found.

He also talked about how the gold would be transported back to Spain.

Detailed information about the second voyage came from one of the passengers. His name was Dr. Diego Alvarez Chanca. He was a physician at the royal court. He wrote a report about the voyage. It is one of the most reliable eyewitness accounts of Spain's first colony. He talked about the native Taíno and Carib peoples. These two groups were enemies. Chanca told about the warfare and violence between them. He also described their agriculture, weaving, and decorative metal work.

Columbus's voyages set the stage for European expansion. But they were poorly planned journeys filled with mistaken ideas, violence, and cruelty. His voyages, and those that came after him, had a devastating effect on the Indigenous people.

A SON'S RESPECT

Around 1538, Columbus's son Fernando Colón, also called Ferdinand Columbus, wrote his father's biography. When he was about 14, he traveled with his father on the fourth voyage. Colón knew how that expedition had ended. When he grew up, Colón became a scholar. He wrote the biography in his father's defense.

Activity
Where in the World?

This book about Columbus mentions many places in the world. On a world map or globe, find each of the ones listed below:

ITALY

PORTUGAL

FRANCE

ENGLAND

SPAIN

ASIA
(or China, India, and Japan)

BAHAMAS

SAN SALVADOR

HAITI

JAMAICA

Learn More

Books

Bader, Bonnie. *Who Was Christopher Columbus?* New York, NY: Penguin Workshop, 2013.

Gunderson, Jessica. *Christopher Columbus: New World Explorer or Fortune Hunter?* North Mankato, MN: Capstone Press, 2014.

Kallen, Stuart. *A Journey with Christopher Columbus.* Minneapolis, MN: Lerner Publications, 2018.

Macdonald, Fiona. *You Wouldn't Want to Sail with Christopher Columbus!* New York, NY: Franklin Watts, 2014.

On the Web

With an adult, explore more online with these suggested searches.

"Christopher Columbus," DK Findout!

"Christopher Columbus Interactive Map," The Mariner's Museum and Park

"Columbus Sets Sail," The History Channel

"Who is Christopher Columbus?" BBC Bitesize

Glossary

administrator (uhd-mih-nuh-STRAY-tuhr) a person in charge of managing something

almanac (OL-muh-nak) a book that predicts the weather for each day and gives facts about the Sun and Moon

circumference (ser-KUM-fruhns) the distance around a curved shape such as a circle or sphere

headwinds (HED-windz) winds that blow opposite of the course of a ship

hostile (HAH-stuhl) feeling or showing great dislike

Indigenous (in-DIH-juh-nuhs) describing the people or animals that originally lived in a certain place

lunar eclipse (LOO-nuhr ih-KLIPS) when Earth passes between the Moon and the Sun, and the Moon is darkened by Earth's shadow

mutiny (MYOO-tuh-nee) a revolt of the members of a ship's crew against the captain or commanding officer

navigator (NAH-vuh-gay-tuhr) a person who charts, sets, and steers the course of a ship

stereotypes (STAIR-ee-uh-tyeps) a simplified idea about a group that is usually untrue or only partially true and is often harmful and insulting

strait (STRAYT) a narrow body of water connecting two larger bodies of water

Index